Printed in the United States of America

Published by

Angel Fergusons'' WordProcessing

Tampa, FL 33617

First Edition

Book Cover Design By James Ferguson III

Library of Congress Cataloging –n– Publication Data

Ordering Information:
Quantity sales. Special discounts are available on quantity
purchases by corporations, associations, and others.

For details, contact the publisher at the address above.
Orders by U.S. trade bookstores and wholesalers.

Please contact

ANGEL FERGUSON'S WORDPROCESSING

angel@angelfergusonswordprocessing.com

Tel: 813.516.4916

Angel Ferguson's Wordprocessing
ISBN-13: **978-0692537756** (Custom)
ISBN-10: **0692537759**
BISAC: **Poetry / Women Authors**

I dedicated this book to the old me who has help me to be who I am today.

To past experiences that made me strong.

I dedicated this to my parents who show me the example of strength and the power of prayer.

I dedicated this to my other half Andrew Tolbert who took me as I am and pushed me to follow my dreams and let the world hear my voice.

To my kids Aliyah, Marcell and Mariyah Tolbert

who I love dearly and help me to know love and taking care of others.

To the man up above for blessing me with the opportunity and giving me the gift.

FAMILY

SISTA

You're part of a man. The better part of him he has said.

You strive for excellence in everything you do.

You're independent because you have been on your own.

Parenting on your own with a baby and no father by your side!

Dark as the night that comes in different shading.

Troubles you overcome because you are a lady!

Shape as a bottle that catches the eyes.

Hips and forms that you can not hide.

The simple of part of men.

Knowledge to be better. Caring and loving to everyone.

You put food in the mouths of every little cub.

Takes care of inside and outside of the home.

Making sure heads pressed and straight all with the ease of a hot comb.

There making sure you know the difference between right and wrong.

There when you need a shoulder to lean on .

There in the beginning when you need a friend.

Black sistas are there till the end.

DEAR MOMMA

I think on days like this the times you spent making me a woman.

Breaking my back and teaching me right from wrong.

Being there when I was sick and all alone.

The only one that was there when daddy was gone.

Suffering through heart ache and pain.

Working daily to keep shelter over heads.

Saying things to make us happy and smile.

Through it all you're worth more than a friend and the greatest gift that God could ever give.

Didn't have much but we made it to the end.

Your love and care I will always need and words won't express what you mean to me.

You're stronger than a rock and braver than a fox and I will always love you.

Dear Momma.........

DADDY

Even though times were hard and you did your best.

You're still a star.

We went through bad times and good ones.

Even though you made bad choices, you still stuck with us and strived to teach us right from your mistakes.

It's hard to faced the past and realize how you hurt your family so bad.

You try to make up the days you miss and bring happiness.

You're not like those other dad's who leave and not come back.

You keep your head up through the storm and rain and say we are going to make it.

Some day we may know a lot of things you don't but it makes you proud and think God for the many blessings you have found.

You don't have to worry, we are praying and hoping for you.

Just know that God will see you through.

I love you daddy.

My Child

Just cause it seem like it's the end, don't mean you can't go on.

You may feel down inside and it makes you want to cry.

Don't mean there won't be sunshine.

Your smile has turn into a frown and your sitting into depression.

Reach out and take my hand because someone understands.

You want to throw something in the air because of all of the drama is in your head.

Breathe, run outside or walk and get some air.

You're low and you feel bad about yourself ,look in the mirror, you're beautiful.

Can't you tell?

You fell alone like everyone has left.

Never forsake me I'm always by your side.

You feel like you can't move on anymore.

I 'll give you a little push to see you through.

I'm only a call away.

My child I am here for you.

IN A BABIES EYES

Dark in the middle of white.

Close, waiting to be seen by light.

Lost in a wondering mind. Images that have never been seen.

Rolling around in my head as I turn to see things that are huge and different.

Shapes and sizes standing around me.

With big bars together flashing at me.

Loud noise around hurting my ears and making me want to cry.

I see this face with big bright eyes like mine.

Those white bars flashing at me again.

With these long pieces of soft strains that feel so soft on my fingers.

I start to pull out.

I hear that loud noise again and try to respond back and noise come out so I think I am talking!

Small fingers and toes taste so good from what I have been shown.

I 'm in another world. Everything is big and small like me.

All these things I see from one little peak!

SISTA TO SISTA

We talk from time to time to tell each other what's on our minds.

You come over or I'll go over to stay the night.

We are two different people.

Two different personalities, that are one of a kind.

We have been there with each other through everything.

Our first boyfriends, first lovers and the first time our hearts were broken.

One tried the first bad thing, you do when you're curious, than tell the other one what it was like!

We were together the first time we became lady's that enter themselves into womanhood, giving someone that big part of you!

We have had fights, ups and downs but it was out of care and love.

We have grown together.

Picked each other up when the other has fallen.

Shared secrets together since we were young and didn't know a thing!

We love each other, have had each other's back.

Because we are not just friends but sistas to the end!

A CHILD

The first time you see them it takes your breath away.

How can something so small and beautiful be in command under you.

Tiny little hands and feet you're so scared to touch because they are so fragile and precious, you don't want to break.

Eyes that look through you.

Say hello again have we met before.

I know your words and you may just look into my eyes.

A smile that can take your breath away.

Like you just know at that moment that everything is okay.

A love that you have never experienced before, one like no other.

A love that even when there is wrong you still smile and sometimes look pass it all.

You say to yourself they are learning still, they're still young.

A gift more precious than gold and piece of your heart & every

mother knows.

My Little Angel Elijah

My little angel I would like to say thank you.

I say thank you cause I don't want to say those other words.

Thank you for letting your presence be known, for the morning sickness just to say mommy I'm getting you ready.

Thank you for the little kicks in the morning and night to say mommy stop tripping or I'm up right now.

Thank you for the talks and listening.

Thanks for stretching my body for 9 months.

I know you're in a better place.

Smiling and laughing right now.

I know you're watching over me and waiting for me to join you.

I know pops is probably holding you and passing you around.

I thank God for the time I was able to share with you and I know He knows what's best.

I love you and even though I am sad I am also glad.

Mommy is going to be ok, just knowing my little angel will be watching over me everyday.

Dedicated to my son Elijah RIP

Family

Family, Family is a group of people that bond.

They stay together in a group.

A family is mostly your mom, dad, brothers & sisters.

But really a family is made up of love within a group of people.

It's like a fist. It has hard times as well as soft ones.

It can break and come back together.

It doesn't matter who is it, it's a group of people that share laughter, sadness, love, strength, pride, courage, going though bad times together as well as good ones.

It's a family!

MY WONDERS

SUNSHINE

My sunshine has risen and the clouds have passed by.

With the touch of his smile and the happiness in his eyes.

He shines a light so bright.

A gift he embraces with words spoken of grace.

Courage inherited from a line of pass on black soldiers.

A love he keeps close with God and for a door to be open.

Fear is shaken with his eyes of bravery.

He strives to always be the best until his soul is at rest.

Golden brown, smooth skin and hands of steel a hardworking man.

My sunshine has risen again.

BAD GIRL

I'm not nice.

I walk by with a twist and curves in my hips, a luscious sweet firm of my backside.

With a big butt perfect breast that matches my little waist and stomach.

With light caramel red skin that catches every eye that walks in.

Reddish brown hair that every female die to get with devil red eyes that will get your fire lit.

You look in my eyes and I'll place you in my spell, you're hot for me I see it in your eyes. I can tell.

You may hear rumors round that I'm not one to tease.

I'm something you have been waiting for, I'm a game.

Once you play me you don't want to leave.

As I touch your hand and rub your leg I know you're going to shake.

I can feel you tremble as I take your breath away I'm in your fantasies to please you with all my naughty ways.

I shock you with my lust of passion of me as I explore you and let you into me.

You want to cry because the feeling of me, feel so good inside.

As you sleep you wake up so suddenly to see that it was just a dream. I'm that good as you can see.

Every man wants me. Every girl is intimidated by me. That's why they hold their man close when they see me.

I'll make you break your promises and leave your girl at home once you come in you're stuck in my dome.

Like I said before I'm not as nice as I may seem.

I'm a DIVA AKA Bad Girl on the scene.

BEAUTIFUL IN THE DARK

Ever seen something so beautiful it just light up your eyes.

Looking at the ocean and wondering how something could be so beautiful in the heat of the night.

How, just when you look at the waves you just see sparkles like stars on top of it.

The moon look like it just lit up the whole world.

It just makes you wonder how God can make something simple as ocean water look so beautiful in a dark sky.

When you look at the water you wonder where it can take you, places you never dream of.

And feeling like you can just fly high in the sky.

How can something so beautiful make you feel the way it do.

Something looking beautiful under the night!

CARAMEL

Caramel that's what I am.

Strong Intelligent! And beautiful!

That's what I am.

I don't let no one put me down.

I'm that independent woman.

That's what I say.

I know what to do in the time of trouble and who to call in the time of need.

Caramel that's my name and Hating is not my game.

I'm that shine in the sun the one that make the men say yummmm when I come!

Thick in the thighs and slim in the waist with a pretty face.

That sunshine

Caramel, that's my name.

FLOWER

Blossoms and grown night and day!

Standing through sunshine and rain

Meaning of strong and brave sadness despite of its way's

Broken for a symbol of love

Torn of a broken heart confesses of love

Dead of hunger and come back to life

It rises again

How beautiful a flower is

LISTEN

Why the wind blow I wonder?

How if you can just listen to it, you hear a whisper of it's sounds.

For if you follow it, it will take you places have or never dreamed of.

I wonder if when you sit in the shade under a tree on a hot sunny day or go to the beach and listen to the ocean you hear wonders of nature talking to you and try to understand what God is trying to tell you.

When you wake up in the morning and step outside the sun shines on your face and you hear the birds like little children circling around the trees.

I think and wonder how life goes as I sit and watch the beautiful days go down I ask myself these questions and wonder if nature will listen to me.

THANK YOU!

Thank you God for I am finally opening up my eyes.

I have no reason to feel bad 4 myself.

I'm beautiful, smart in my own way, creative, artistic, have goals in life.

And no matter how hard or how long it takes I'm going to make it through as long as I have you.

Now I know I have a reason for living.

You said not to cry over spoiled milk and no weapon formed against me shall prosper.

I'm sorry 4 not coming to you in the first place instead of worrying about some boy.

Somebody always told me don't think you have it so bad because somebody may have it worse than you!

I always held my head up high and you brought it to my eyes.

Always gave good advice instead of taking it myself.

I always know these battles are yours and not mine.

I should love myself because I know you love me!

Please help me see clearer from my heart and soul.

Fix my mind and take my heart and soul.

My mother and grandmother always told me to pray when I was feeling down because you would always be around.

You are my shepherd and no harm should come towards me.

Thank you for always being there for me.

TIME

I tried to hurry my time was running out.

I only had an hour left and I can hear the ticking sound.

The hand on the clock was moving as my eyes followed it.

The red hand was going round and round as sweat from my face was pouring down.

Only one thing was on my mind and that was not to waste any time.

The sun looked like it was about to go down as night was approaching.

The sky changed his color my eyes twitched and I knew the moon was about to light.

I only had minutes left.

I wish the time would stop.

It seemed as if it was going faster than before.

I realized I had no time anymore.

My time ran out.

I was too late now I have to sit in this grave and wait.

A CHANGE

A new beginning is about to come as this separation becomes life.

I ask myself a question since the conversation has arose in my hear!

It is for good or for bad but I don't know it seems as though I really don't care but he is a part of my life even though it seems he's not always there.

So will I miss him or will I be in the same faze that it doesn't matter, I have been without him anyway.

But it was not forever.

Will this time be so that is a big thing to think about!

Will I need the image of a role model in my life?

I know others that have made it without them but I also know others who never had them.

I was blessed enough to have that image in my life so should I be grateful for that and not think of all the bad times.

I mean I'm not a boy so maybe it won't be so bad.

I have grown up now, made my own decisions but he the other half.

I feel him when he's doing wrong.

I always have since one night when I was young.

Lil brother might take it hard he's always saying I don't know about this one!

But I feel like I can't say the same it's just something in me that won't feel pain. I guess because I have seen my mother go through so much heart ache and pain.

It seems like her stormy cloud won't go away.

So I have learned to be strong in these days and times.

I will always love him even though I can cry a tear of pain.

LOVE & KINDNESS

Love is something a person share. It's something from the heart.

Kindness is sweet words from the mouth like love it comes from the heart.

Something so sweet can mean so many things. It can open your eyes and teach you something.

Chase your stormy clouds away. Put a smile on your face when you're wearing a frown.

Bring you happiness when you're feeling down. Love and kindness is a mixture of joy to me.

It keeps you alive and on your feet. Nothing can replace the love and kindness God has given me.

The precious gift he has given me I spread to others as they spread it to me.

Love is a word God gives in so many ways .

Spiritually, physically and emotionally.

The kindness we share in those ways .

Without kindness we don't have love .

That's why love and kindness is a gift from God in so many ways.

Love is a gift we can't lose but we can choose.

Kindness we should give to all.

Feelings we feel despite the mind but from your heart.

We are brothers and sisters in Christ cause God loves us all.

Kindness we sometimes share from the mind and heart.

Love and kindness should always come from within cause you never know when it's the end.

NOT THERE

Why do people make it seem like they are happy when they really not?

Smile , you see on the outside.

It's really a frown within.

Trying to ease the tears inside so no one won't be suspicious.

You feel like you're missing something and you don't know what it is!

So why should I be happy when I'm just fronting, pretending!

People looking at you wanting to know what's on your mind cause you making mean faces while you're walking through the crowd.

They say you have changed but it's not for the good.

You're always mad and mean like someone has hurt you.

But I show how I feel.

Why should I be happy when it's not for real?

Little laughs come now and then but it will soon disappear.

I feel I'm missing something but don't know what it is.

HANGING OUT

Just getting to school and the bell hasn't rang.

Big crowds of people standing around.

As I walk around the school, sitting at the table talking with some of my friends laughing and joking around about yesterday and what we did.

After school is another time of fun boys be booming and flowing about someone.

People gathering around and listen to listen to the tunes.

Couples hugging and kissing saying " good bye I'll see you soon"

This is how we hang out in high school.

DON'T JUDGE ME OF MY SKIN!

Don't judge me from my skin color.

If my skin is light like butter and tan like caramel.

Don't judge me as white, mix or Hispanic.

If I am smooth brown and dark like chocolate.

Don't see me as a tar or black.

If I'm light skin or red, don't call me white girl or mix girl.

Call me the light because if my butter soft tan caramel silky skin.

In the light that your eyes has cast upon.

If I'm dark don't call me tar baby or burnt.

Call me the night for my dark sexy brown chocolate skin.

I'm the night that you call beautiful.

So judge me on my intelligence, my personality and courage not because of my skin color.

Because I'm the one that's going to shine.

RED ROSE

Red Rose, Red the color of what I am.

Rose a flower that I smell like.

When it blossom and glows.

I blossom and grew beautiful!

That's what it is.

That's what people say.

Red a color that can be expressed as so many things.

Red a flower stands.

It has a lot of meanings.

One of the meanings is to remember.

But if you look at it, it's something that can't be explained.

Just like life.

To use Red Rose is the meaning of beautiful.

FACE TO FACE

You're back in my life. Could this be right?

I see your warm faces and smiles of happiness.

It seem right or am I wrong.

My face is full with expressions as I sit and think about it.

Wondering if my mind and spirit was my heart telling me right.

Or was I confused with passion of untrue love.

Was I beaten in anger and scared to face the truth that lies in my face?

Maybe I was hiding from bitterness and pain in the world I face.

I think back the time when you used to show the light and I thought I was doing right.

Where did I go wrong was I placed in the pit of sadness?

Or an imaginary world?

The pitch of an wide feeling I have upon myself.

Where do I go now?

Do I try to face the heads of time?

I'm lost and need to be found.

Save me from the image I have found.

WORDS

Words can be harsh and words can be mean.

Words can make you say something's you don't mean.

Words can make you cry from happiness and joy.

Words can make you love someone you don't even know things that come out your mouth to show feeling.

Words you can't express and has no meaning.

Words can be dull and words can be powerful, words can be worth more than gold.

DREAM

Dreams of hope.

Dreams of steel!

Dreams that you will never worry again.

Sleeping in silence, whisper of words.

Images coming to life from single phrases.

Bad things that happen and bad things you see.

In your face with one little peak.

World of world and world of dream.

How can you tell reality when it all seems the same to me.

Pictures in your mind and when you open your eyes, your dream can be signals or visions with a meaning.

It's like a riddle or a puzzle to solve.

You don't know where you begin or fall.

A dream can be a dream or nothing at all.

WAKE UP CALL

Wake up the world is calling you, can't you hear it?

It's loud and clear are you blinded by the faults of everyday life?

Where do you stand in this world of hate.

Has your back been beaten with the words of shame.

Do you dream of one day howling flame.

Is your life nothing more than a lie.

Do you cry.

Does it hurt to try?

Are you sleep with your shoes on ready to fight waiting for the sunlight to shine bright .

Are you afraid to live. Afraid to give.

Could you stare in your soul mates eyes and say good bye without knowing why?

If this poem can relate to you well you need to wake up.

Wake up because your wake up call is calling you!

MUSIC

As a child sounds came clear

Music the only thing I wanted to hear.

I thought about what music meant.

It's more than just a beat or tap.

Music the sound the rhythm of the beat!

The sound of trumpets playing

Drums beating to the melody.

People stand and dance as they hear the tones that make them tap their feet.

I think about it more as I am older.

It makes you want to jump up as your feet feel it in your hips as they curve and your shoulders bouncing and you twirl all around.

You feel like you're high, high in the sun and you're a beautiful as a butterfly.

Songs that make your voice go high as the echo follows the tone.

Music with different meaning like R &B. Music for your soul!

That's when you hear it.

Makes you want to cry cause it's talking about you and I.

Music that makes you fall in love.

Think about good times that's been gone.

Music is all around you, it's in the air and sky.

LOOKING BACK

It's funny how when you're born you think you have all the answers.

You know what you want to be.

You want to a singer, policemen or a princess.

As time goes by your decision may change or they may still be the same.

It depends on how you main-tame.

It is funny how things always go the opposite way then what you want it to be.

You may find yourself to be a different person than what you thought you would be.

When times get rough and you have tough times on your hands , you may find yourself struggling.

Dreams you had as a child you forgot about.

Left it in the pass because you realize they may never happen.

As you look ahead you don't see anything bright.

You look and hear about other people's lives, you sit and say to your-self, must be nice!

LIFE

Unborn to light with a mind of it's own.

Thought of words that you have been told.

Spreading in body but not in soul.

Knowing image and imagination but not the real world.

Free we are but we still have chains.

Smiles on everyone faces but there are tears within.

Money something to look at to break the thought of being poor.

Choices you make to choose what side you are on.

Wrong definition everybody does.

Skin the different shades to show you are.

Strength we are taught, weakness is not an acceptance.

Courage we get when we strive to achieve.

Belief s hard when we face personalities.

Heart what we follow as our guide.

Outlook what we don't see because we are blind.

Love we have to help us move on.

Emotion a mixture of what you feel inside.

Pain a lesson of everyday life.

ODE TO THE OCEAN

Ode to the ocean.

I can hear you through the breeze.

Your soft wind that gaze upon you puts my mind to sleep.

As I look at you flowing so calmly I wonder what images you have seen and what distance you have traveled.

I see your pattern as you change colors from day to night.

When the sun goes down you have such a beautiful image of orange and yellow bright but delightful.

When the sky gets dark you're nice to look at under the night light stars.

Ode to the ocean.

I can hear your whispers in my ear saying it's going to a beautiful day because the sky is clear when you are near.

I can close my eyes as I listen to you and I feel like I'm in another world.

Ode to the ocean.

I am here take me with you.

AT HOME

You really surprised me.

Something inside has broken free.

I thought it was going to be good because you can be better than the other.

You were impressive at first, surprises and heart warm times.

But now you have grown into a deeper level.

Usually you expect that the good times always come first.

It starts out as fun but then you know it leads into a disaster.

That's when the thought comes in, the fun is over and it lasted while it could. It's time to move on.

But when this started I knew something inside of me telling me this is much more.

I didn't want to believe that so I kept it closed inside of trying to ex-plore.

I t took me to old places where I was over whelmed to a point but did-n't go any further.

Than I realized I was fronten, fooling myself cause now I have a better offer.

I'm impressed but happy at what my heart has chosen.

I feel it knows it's place and where its going.

Till it finds it's space at home.

F.A.T

I'm not the normal thing as you may see.

You see I have a little more extra that's why I'm so unique.

My thighs are thick and juicy.

My backside is big and round even if it's not sticking out.

My arms usually have a extra tan to them.

I come in different shapes and tone.

I might be tall so it seems like I have more up top than bottom.

I might be short with a lot all around.

You see me everywhere you go.

I'm the one that catches every eye when I walk in the door.

I'm the one you are afraid of and give you a bad impression.

You stereo type me but don't know what's within.

You call me names like it's a crime to be juicy on the outside.

I'm bot worried though because I'm beautiful in and out.

I'm coming back it's my time to shine.

A beautiful plus size queen has arrived.

SCHOOL

I think about things that's going on at school and in my household.

Mainly about the stress and struggle just to make it to the 12th grade.

In high school I have to take test just to test my mentality.

To see if I belong in a certain level or this place call school.

Raising scores to make it harder for passing.

Laughing in your face because they know you're going to fail like you did before.

I push myself a little more and try not to believe the negativity they tell me everyday.

Than I think about my life, what I'm going to do when I'm through.

I'm stuck with a hard decision of if I want to go through this again.

If I don't go to college will it really have a big effect on me.

Will it hurt me or my family.

Will they look at me different.

I mean I don't know if it's the thing for me!

PRINCE

A prince us what we see in fairy tales.

Someone who is a figure f a real man.

Someone who is smart, sweet and fine!

The three main words in one.

Every girl has a prince, a man that will sweep her off her feet.

I want one who can be funny, don't take things so serious.

Knows how to enjoy the fine things in life.

A man I can tell anything, who understands me.

As well as when I fall and have up's and downs.

A best friend as well as a lover.

Built with tight abs and a cute face with dreads.

That's my ideal man.

My prince in my fairy tale.

Once day we will get our prince.

We may not get the full thing but some thing close to it.

My favorite fairy tale is Cinderella.

I would love to be her any day.

BABY GIRL

Girls I see you walking by.

You look a mess and like you're down inside.

Trying to find answers but you don't know why.

People saying things going through one ear and coming out the other.

Baby girl I know it's hard and you feel like you want to give up at times.

But all you have to do is keep your head up high.

Baby girl they want you to fall that's why you don't let them get to you. And stand tall!

Baby girl a man is not the answer to your problems he can only comfort you but he is not going to struggle with you.

Baby girl you will be left there in your anger and pain.

Baby girl as a African Queen we were taught how to deal with these things.

Baby girl you have your strength , faith and God to guide you through your way!

Baby girl you're a growing woman that have others who go through are feeling the same way!

GRAD

I have walked across the stage.

Heart pounding and breathing fast.

I was scared but I stood tall and was brave.

I finally made it to the end.

But it still hasn't hit me that I will no longer see friends, teachers and the sign that says Tampa Bay Tech High no longer

when I open my eyes.

I have made it to the end, no more school for me.

I just don't feel it though.

It really hasn't hit me that I have entered into adulthood.

When people ask me how I feel I don't know what to say.

I feel normal I don't know what I can say.

I won't know until I really see that I have finally graduated.

THINK

When I think of the past.

Old love one's old things I laugh at how crazy things were then.

Growing up thinking I always had it bad and why I was always so sad.

I try to think how things I thought would happen didn't.

When you think things out it all seem so different.

The world can change before your eyes.

How can you predict the future as it change.

How do you know what's going to happen.

Superstations comes from your thoughts.

The world can end at any.

Days, change one after another.

You can't go back in time or change the weather.

All you can think of is how strange.

Life is your days are counted don't wasn't them over nothing.

WHY I SMILE

I smile because I am happy

I smile because I'm free

I smile because no one can do harm to me.

I smile because the sun rises on my face and I can see another day.

I smile because God has bless me with many things.

I smile to express my joy and hide my pain.

I try to smile in stormy clouds and rain.

Cause I know trouble don't last always.

I smile through the day and night

I smile because I'm not afraid

I smile because I have strength

I smile because I have won my voice

I smile 4 the one that can't

I smile from within.

LEARNING

UNDERSTAND ME

I'm the same when you look at me but different in a way.

My feelings are strong and expressions don't explain them.

No could ever imagine the things I think or never alone think that those things come to mind.

Silence is what I do best to stay straight and what I do to stay in place.

I try to keep happy and do things to have joy.

I am a depressed person. I don't do the things that I think for if I do I wouldn't be in this world.

My feelings and mind I can't understand, most people can do or say what's on their minds and react to their feelings.

I can't. No one understand me not even my own mother so I don't talk about my sorrow or share my feelings.

I sit in bed and weep like a child. I wonder and imagine things, things that a three year old wonder when it's trying to figure out something or watching a Disney movie, I'm not good at school work but I try to do my best.

I'm good at giving people advise except for myself.

That's what I don't understand. I write poetry when something come to my mind.

I guess that's one of my I explain in what I think but don't know about feelings.

I write things I think to get it off my mind.

Some ways I get from daddy.

Others I don't know.

Trying to figure me out if you can.

SHOCK

The hand of my lover left a mark on my face.

The redness and anger in his eyes made me want to run away.

The man I knew before, I no longer see.

The man I thought I would spend my life with, turned his back on me.

Took my love now I have nothing left but shame as I look at myself.

As the deepness in his voice became higher my emotions took over my as my fist physically took place.

That I left a red mark on his face.

My heart pounding as I tried to calm down.

My eyes looked at his.

We were both in tears, realized the anger we just went through.

The madness in me made me walk away.

I still can't believe that happened until this day.

TOUCHED

Touch by an finger. Whisper in ear.

Tears rolled down my eyes. I'm sitting down shaking with fear.

Words I'm trying to make out cause I don't understand them.

Images I wish I could see in this dark, dark place.

Red puddles of water flowing down my face.

Pain I'm feeling inside that I can't erase.

I'm praying on my knees to let me see another day.

Please don't let me be scattered in bones laying in a grave.

A mental peace goes to my head as I close my eyes.

Peace of my flesh torn as I see eyes.

My body quenched as I felt the soul of me cast away.

I'm no longer a woman.

The touch if a finger took that away.

STRESS

Stress on my mind, mind of stress and all I want to do is put my soul at rest.

Too much on my mind and I can't deal with it.

I have no one to help me, all they do is pile on more stress.

Crying cause I'm lost and my mind is gone.

I'm hurting inside and trying to be strong.

But I've been wasted with the things you used to make me happy and have a good time.

But with all this stress and weakness that's the only thing on my mind.

I'm showed love and there's hate in this world.

You find someone to chill with and then someone to look out for,

All this I have to think about and then much more.

I write but not good in school.

Breaking hearts and not doing so good.

Stress pile up on tress.

Someday I wish all this stress will rest.

CHAPTER

A chapter that should I close.

I'm stuck between should I leave and let go.

He has his friends and everything is cool.

He doing his own thing I sometimes feel like I'm intruding!

I don't fit in maybe, I should leave them alone!

Find my own friends and a place I can go.

He sweet and I love him but I think I should give him his space.

At home it's another chapter that I open too many times.

I shouldn't even go there!

Maybe I should leave them both alone.

I should go out of town and be on my own.

Maybe I'm an outsider, I don't belong in either one of these chapters!

I should make my own that includes me!

WAS LOST BUT NOW I AM FOUND

Was lost for a while buried under life.

New this. New that.

No time for you.

Hope for that time to find you again.

Not realizing how much you were missed.

You were a part of something to make it through.

Through emotions, tuff times, heart aches.

I needed you.

When I put you down everything clashed and I felt like where do I turn too.

But back then when there was no left or right there was you.

Forgive me for your misplacement.

I'm finding my way back in due time.

Maybe it was I who needed you when I needed you like I need you like I do now.

Now that we have met again this new relationship has given me a smile.

It's something that I really needed to brighten up that dark cloud.

Hello again it has been a while.

TIRED CHARACTER

Tired of words being spoken not being heard.

Tired of carrying luggage and heavy loads off of everyone else's carriage.

Go to everyone stop sign where it says full no room to leave baggage here!

When they need you, you're always there.

When you need then you find no room there,

Took all your good bags and gave them away to replace someone else's.

Being different characters to make others happy instead of yourself.

Which role am I playing today is something you often say a lot.

When is it going to be time when I find my character that is wife in wanting to come out again.

That role hasn't been cast yet I see!

Tired of carrying, bending over backwards cause all they want to do is make me the bag lady!

Tired of playing the bag lady character.

These bags are getting heavy and heavier.

What happen when there is no more room and this character has been dropped from the cast! (not been casted)

TIRED

I'm not the person I want to be.

I find myself being somebody that not truly me.

I'm still hiding behind this image you know that is yours.

Not showing my true feelings but being there for yours.

When I finally do I finally do I'm happy again and everything is ok with me and you.

When you still don't get it and I'm tired of giving clues.

When is it going to be me and you.

I have sat and waited all the time.

Even turned other good offers because I love you and you're mine.

What I don't understand is why I hold on when I am hurting all the time.

The only time you have for me is when sex is on your mind, It's like I only appear when football is not around.

Well if that's the case then why am I around?

Cause I know I'm barely on your mind.

When I call you, you're mad that it's my voice on the other end line and tired all the time.

I'm tired of this fake image for U of mine.

I want to be free or for you to just notice me.

I'M LOST

I'm lost, lost in love, lost in school, lost in the world.

A question was asked, Do you feel like you belong in the world?

I ask myself that question. I feel like I belong but I don't know what for.

Sometimes I feel like I don't belong.

I just don't care anymore. I don't know what I want to do.

I have been told and criticized about being dumb.

That I really start to believe that I am. I can't spell and get picked on about my mentality.

I'm ghetto talking with no sense and not all there.

Basically I want you to see these girls that are immature and don't know what to with their life, I feel if that's what people see me as that really know me is that what I should be.

Men see as a person I don't see, not even my family.

This other person that's smart has a great personality and s beautiful with a sexy body.

It's nice to know but it's not me. I'm a drama queen, I act as if I have more worse than everybody when there is a lot of people have it worse than me.

I just have a lot of questions and don't know the true me. I'm 17 years old and don't know what I want to be in life and I 'm going to be some-body. I feel like I'm 30 and treated like I'm 13, I don't even know what it is like to be a teenager, my time is almost up.

As for as love goes I'm in love bit I can't be. I have to hid it because they say I'm too young and am moving too fast. I don't need to be into boys too soon.

So what's the use because of that I have issues and don't know what to do. I'm lost give me a clue.

3 WORDS

<u>EMOTIONS</u> – The need to see, feel and hear the one your heart calls. The tiny puddle of water that falls down your cheeks when you are down on the ground and you realize you have fell. The frustration you build up in your head to hold your anger until you explode. A woman's gift's what makes her strong and what she stands upon.

<u>LOVE</u>- Words that we say all the time, but only we know if they are true. One thing your heart guides you too but can make you confused. A hard situation that can be a fairytale or a tragedy. It depends on what you make your ending to be. Your mother and God's love is the strongest love there will ever be.

<u>GROWING</u>- Knowing right from wrong and the choices you make. Realizing your mistakes and learning from the lessons they teach. Not doing or having the same mentality that you had as you were young. Knowing life is a lesson to lean and you just have to get through and make it to the end.

CRY

A feeling in making my stomach that is so deep.

Makes my heart drop and my insides want to say words.

Makes my toes tingle as the same feeling goes through my feet.

Make your eyes water like they have been feel with buckets of rain.

Your cheeks turn red like paint and you feel the feeling that can only be shown as a expression.

Red eyes the color of fire that need to be turn to smoke.

This feeling can be like a glass that has been broken.

You feel like you finally are free.

Shield up for so long you realize that sometimes you just have to let go.

Silence of a dark cloud in the sky.

Wanting to scream out for someone to hear the sound.

Letting it all out at one time.

A feeling I feel when I cry.

FEELING DOWN

As I look back on everything, I didn't think I would be here.

I thought I had it together, yea at first I was surprised I made it this far but now it seem like my hard work has come to an end.

I'm out of school and I'm doing nothing.

I have no job and I didn't go to college.

I feel worthless like I'm nothing.

Everything people said was right.

It's said when you're out of school and doing nothing with your life.

My mother always said I was just like my father and it turned out she was right.

I 'm in my house caged up like a animal wanting to break free.

Want to go somewhere but can't.

Want to do something but instead sleep and eat all day.

Get yelled at cause they say you're worthless and think you don't have to do anything with your life cause you don't at least have a job.

I never thought I would be in this boat and I hope one day I would get of it.

FALLEN

Rain drops fall as a symbol of my tears.

Lighting flash has the anger in my eyes were shown.

A load of me has dropped into a hole.

Bitterness of a face that has not been seen.

Silence in a place where a mouth has been closed.

Dark for night hopping for light to be shown.

Fire lite for a heart that's been burned.

A soul that's lost and looking for return.

A rose that shed for the days that pass.

Dirt and soil the color of my skin.

A chair rocking that I am falling in.

FINDING MYSELF

ATTENTION

All I wanted was for someone to notice me.

Not for my looks and body but for what I like to do, what keeps me happy.

For someone who's supposed to be with me tell me they love me as well as show me.

Not tell me you love me and only show me when your inside of me.

I never got a gift from a boy on my birthday.

Only received 1 gift for Christmas and it was torn.

Never got a gift for Valentines' Day but I had a Valentine, you can say.

My parents love but they didn't seem to show interest unless my grades went down.

But not when it came to what I like doing.

They said it won't make any money to many people doing it.

When it came to my lil brother they fell in love.

My boyfriend is not there, he has his mind on sports and family, so there's no attention for me.

All I needed was attention but no one really gave it to me so, I'm like all alone since no one really sees me. I keep to myself.

Sometime I try not to be seen.

It's not like anyone cares cause no one really has shown any attention to me.

ANOTHER ROUND

I got you but at times I feel I need some space.

When things are not straight I need some time to sit and think.

It's kind of strange because either way I still feel lonely every day.

I need someone to talk to. Someone to comfort me.

To hold me in their arms. To caress my body.

To put their big strong black arms around me while they whisper in my ear.

A girl gets lonely and is afraid of being alone.

But a girl is also tired of going through the same crape over and over again.

Tired of breaking hearts, being mixed up and don't know which way to go.

Tired of writing about men and the problems I have with them.

So I guess I got to take it slow………………………….

2LOVERS

Am I ready for love.

I'm confused and don't know where my heart is leading me.

Feelings I have for one I have for another.

Don't know what to say my lips are sealed with pressure.

My mind is telling me one thing and someone is telling me another.

I loved you but you left.

BETWEEN DIRECTIONS

It's hard when you think you have everything planned out and something changes your whole mind set.

You get lost between,

attitudes,

morals,

actions

and

words people betray.

WHAT I THINK I SHOULD BE

People ask me how do you see yourself in 10 years?

What does your future hold?

I ask myself that same question and think about it for a while.

But the thing is I came up with two different side.

One side I see is not a good image.

Yeah going to school but doing something for money is not what I love.

Partying all night long doing things I didn't and couldn't do when I was young.

Reliving the part of wondering what its like in teenage days.

But I become stuck in that phase.

The other side is good going to school not doing what I love but eventually that comes soon making my book and showing the world what I see, marrying my soul mate who means the world to me.

Living good, wealthy and healthy life because my husband has fulfilled his dreams.

My mind saying I won't be with him one on one side cause it all fails because of my curiosity.

So I am hoping for the second one but you never know what your future holds.

So all I can do right now is let the days pass by and grow old.

FINDING HERSELF

Search is easy to do but deep down inside is something to think about .

Reality is in the mix of imagination.

So how do we know the real world and the things that last upon it.

Do we really know our selves like we say we do or do we just think we know our selves by the things we do.

Think about it!

DECISION

We both did wrong now we have to suffer the consequences .

We let our hormones and passion take over us and didn't think nothing would happen.

Even though we didn't use our heads the first time instead we did the same thing over again.

Now I am stuck with a test and don't know if it's positive yet.

I want to make the biggest mistake but in the future I know I will regret it.

I want to bring a life in this world.

But a baby having a baby will be so wrong.

I feel it would bring me joy.

I will give it love I haven't gave and gotten before.

But a career and education it may take me from.

I'm stuck with my conscious telling me different things.

Bringing someone in this world, I'm not shame.

I don't know I think I'm stuck in the love game.

But this is one thing I plan I will do it someday!

I'M SORRY

I left one day because I had to get myself straight.

I lied and said that It was because of you but it was because

I couldn't explain the truth.

I was drinking to erase my pain. Running from any stress that came. Going with someone else made it worse.

I was emotionally abused and I could face it anymore.

So I thought running would be best.

But I realized I had to stand up and face it myself.

You can't help someone when you can't help yourself.

Or give someone love when you have non left.

I know I left you all alone. Your heart broken and torn.

I'm begging for you to let that go.

I regret it everyday, missing your face.

Pain inside and there's an empty space.

I looked in another's eyes and it didn't seem the same.

The hurt of my lover came back in return.

The abuse from another came to me as tears rolled down your eyes.

I pray that you can forgive me someday.

I'm making it up for all those days from 2004 till the end.

Anything you need I am always here.

I hope you can count on me.

I'm sorry I will never leave again.

MY POWER

The thing I cherish most of all I let fall.

The thing that kept me happy day and night.

The thing I wouldn't give you without a fight was gone.

And I couldn't get it back anymore.

My feelings, my words the only thing I had is this life was my

power.

The strength, power, spirit of me.

The only thing that would not le me down.

The only thing that make my future go around.

The one that show how real I am and that I'm not a phony.

The only thing that can do something 4 me.

What I have used to reach out to the world.

Words that made people think what I feel.

Words you can relate to in your mind.

Words I use to touch a heart, broken and torn.

What I used to explain myself to others.

What I am in soul and flesh.

My words is power and there not gone yet.

MY FIGHT

You think you got me but I'm not gone yet.

I don't give up easy I'm here for more..

No weapon formed against me and this battle is not yours.

I have fallen down once or twice but I'm back up again.

I have been through storm and rain and I'm struck by lighting torn apart.

Went over the valley's and hills and you haven't broke me yet.

You do what ever you want but I'm still staying strong.

This rainy cloud won't last long.

I still have my sword and shield and I'm still going to fight until I win.

Whenever you want to do this again I'll still be here.

Just let me know cause I'm here till the end.

SILENCE

There's a lot I have to tell you but don't know how to start.

All my words I put together but they won't come out.

Things are not what the same and I feel alone everyday.

I don't want to say anything cause you will think I just complain.

I think if I tell you how I feel that you won't listen and take it the wrong way.

But the way you have changed I can't tell you anyway.

I feel like a wife and her husband is overseas and she's sitting there waiting for him to come to her soon.

Hoping he's ok and knowing he has a lot to do.

I always will be there supporting you through the end.

But I just want you to taker a right turn before you come to a dead end.

So I'll just won't say anything until I find a way.

I'll just let you do your same routine, leave everyday.

A TURN

Your brown eyes, light caramel skin and reddish hair brings out the best in you.

You're new to the world and have some growing to do.. You started out goofy, exploring new things.

Playing outside, getting muddy but didn't care about the rain. Now you're 11 and your women has come. It's a start for you, you're about to be a teenager.

So you think you know everything. What you don't know is you are about to go through a big change. You're 13 and now you don't act the same. Your smile has turn into a frown and boys are on your mind. Liking is one thing but moving further is another.

You're 14 and your body is starting to form. You now have breast and body parts that you choose to show. What you don't know is the mind of men and the bets they plan miss innocent can be turned into a hoe! Just by the sayings of one mouth. You don't have to be sleep-ing around to have your clothes you out there.

You're in high school now, 15 and its time to face reality. Time to go through your changes. The pressure you're going to face. Growing too fast and forgetting your place. Didn't know the danger you can get in and the chances you take. Things you have to do to please a boy. Mad at the world, thinking you have nothing to fall back on. Mad at yourself and everyone else. So you had sex to change it all. You keep going instead if stopping. Didn't know what was going through your system.

You are 16 now, you realize you still a child but it doesn't matter you have a baby now. Should have realized what was coming. Instead of sitting down crying. Now becoming something you should have been. Teach your children what to do and what you shouldn't do. Now it's time to make a U-turn and start all over again.

A IMAGE I HAVE TO LET GO!

I have been wanting to get this off my chest for as long as I can re-member. Since I have been young I have been seen as the one that's not so smart, gullible, don't know where your mind be and the one people will take for granted. I have always been called these things and I have started to believe it. I saw myself as dumb and stupid. Re-ally, I made an image for myself around the people who saw me that way. I felt I wasn't getting any support when I needed it, when I was in after school programs, yea they bragged about it for a minute. But only went to one game and convert. So I just started quitting because I felt why do it when there's no one there to cheer me on. At school they worried about me when the teacher called and said I was doing bad. But I didn't care because I felt like they thought. That was the best I could do anyway. I don't have any brains. When it came to graduate, everybody was there. It was the biggest event of the year because they didn't think the girl with no brains would make it. So because of this I turned to boys for my comfort because they thought I was smart. They boasted my head up and supported me in what I was doing. So I lost my innocence early. I have always felt like leaving and there has been many times when I wanted to run away. Go to someone where no one knew me and I could just be free. Now I have made it this far and look where it has gotten me. I have no job and I'm not furthering my education. I'm a sad case because I have always tried to do what my parents have said. This is not how I saw myself. This is not where I want to be. But I'm not going to let it ruin me. It's all good. I will just support me!

SOMETHING TO EASE MY MIND

Something to ease my mind to make me think of a time.

A time when I felt free and nothing could worry me.

A time of laughter and peace, like when its spring time.

When fresh air is surrounding you like a garden of flowers.

Something to put my mind at ease, something that when you just think about it a smile is on your face long before you know it.

Like ice cream when it's hot outside, just to cool your mouth off.

Something to put your mind at ease like the joy of love when you feel like you're on cloud 9, flying so high.

Something to ease my mind, like that first kiss that you've been waiting on for such a long time.

You feel like you're playing hop- scotch and you finally made it to the end.

Something to ease my mind.

To take away that thump of pain ringing in the back before the next thing that pops up and worries you.

Something to ease my mind. I try to go think of a time

WHAT I WANT 2 SAY

It's a lot I want to say that's in my head everyday but I can't because everyone will have something to say and will take it the wrong way.

I would like to say how I feel about everything and how I see it.

What I don't like and what I feel should change.

What I think would help me.

To let people know why I act the way I do.

To tell the truth that I put on a fake image all the time.

That this so called happy girl is really dying inside.

To stand up and show everyone and don't care because I said what I felt and that's what I thought about it.

Instead of saying in my head all the time and keeping everything to myself.

To get it all out I write it down, that's why poems tell a story!

How I see things and maybe what I've been through.

I think one day, everything is going to come out when I have a breakthrough.

LEARNING

How to do something for the first time and wondering if you would get to know how to do it.

Doing something but it doesn't work, so you keep trying.

Getting mad because it just doesn't turn out the way you want it too.

Thinking of how to tell someone something without hurting their feelings.

Knowing you did something wrong and you have to fix it.

Knowing what's wrong and you will get in trouble if you do it again. Meeting new people, getting used to personalities.

Realizing that it's a struggle out in the world.

Making changes just to pass through.

Loving someone but knowing it's not going to work out and breaking their heart will be what you do.

A skill we learn to do. Learning is a process of life.

You have the courage but are afraid to take actions because of the display of different things everyday.

But if you don't take seems as if you're giving up once again.

Is this my fight to win the mind ponders on, yet you get told it's not and move on.

Signs of others showing you a different road. Which way should I go.

Torn between directions and heavy loads.

Is it a road block am I supposed to go around and redirect my navigation? Or am I to supposed to turn left to get to right?

The questions that ponder where and how to miss right!

LEFT OUT

Ever feel like you are in a imaginary world.

You see things and can feel everything but it seems as if it's not there.

Like everything around you is moving but you are standing still.

Like no one notices you and you're screaming inside but no can hear.

You feel like you have been trapped in a box and you have been there for years.

When it seems like things are getting better they become bad again.

You realize that you're used to it so you act as if you're invisible.

You feel invisible from everything, the pain and the anger.

So your best suggestion is to run away.

Cause it feels like you're away anyway!

To feel free from this world of imagery even though it really is real.

But how can it be real when you feel dead.

There's only oxygen to show that you are alive on the outside.

You're lost in words don't know what to say, tired of the same thing. It's a repeating of things that changes at it's own pace.

So you don't care about anything and you want to go away.

LOSING

There it goes again, that feeling once again I'm put in that space.

It's always the same routine I find something then I find you.

I know its only about a matter of time before you show up.

It's good at first, I like it. I've gotten all of these ideas and I'm going to get started.

Things start showing there faces and don't go as planned. Here comes a doubt, I don't know if this is for me again.

Then here comes reasons and pro's and con's.

Seems like the con's are the winner.

You're getting close my friends. Quitter! Quitter, you're not a winner.

So you take the shorter route.

This navigator is classier but at the end you knew all along you were supposed to take the other route.

Start again and you have come back my friend. Quitter! Quitter you're not a winner.

Here we go again.

Depp down you're fighting to win but your appearance, your view is different to the naked eyes.

Won, No you have not.

A ANGEL

When an angel goes to sleep it wakes up gracefully.

It's always at God's right hand.

All dressed in white, trying to make everything right.

Coming in your time of trouble.

Beautiful as a twinkle little star.

Looking down on the one's that fall picking them up as they stumble and crawl.

Everyone has one in the sky above.

Maybe right in front of your face and you don't even know it yet.

An angel doesn't have to be in the sky all the time it can be a loved one or as a friend of an y kind.

A angel is a kind of heart filled with love, a caring spirit and that you can always count on.

An angel comes from within you.

WONDERING ******

Not knowing wondering why having the answers for others and not having a answer for me. I'm not supposed to know the answer or am I afraid. Am I to much for everyone including myself. Anger I have to much but no one knows it because it's covered up by skin. Disappointment I have so much it's my friend. So many thoughts running around my head to go further to try and meet its satisfaction. Satisfaction is messing me up and the one's around me and I know it. Greed for more it's more to the story. This way that way. Am I crazy and don't know it? Am I only sane to myself? They push me away tell me you can do it , look at me like I'm crazy but say that it's love. Do it really feel like that I see a smile on your face but on the inside of mine there is a frown. I can't say nothing. Quiet. I have to be. They can't be around me and keep their insanity. Am I different to the normal. I understand what am called but I know what's up ahead where will I go to fail. It is not easy now and I'm in this one man stand. Help then who are going to help me. Being strong is carrying weight that is to heavy. I am still human. I am still a person. I don't know maybe they don't see. My feelings are trying to take over me. The mind wonders, it never skips a beat. Emotions crying saying save me.

FLYING

I'm flying and no one's around.

There are 2 ways I can go but I don't know which one to take.

I have made choices on my own but now I'm lost and don't know which one to take.

I'm alone and running a raced. I left behind everything that came my way. I'm still flying but I'm not free.

Something is holding me down and trying to take me.

I feel like chains are on my feet and I can't get free.

I'm tired of trying, of turning and wiggling in different directions cause it's not helping me.

So I stop and wait until I can see ahead of me as the chains I have loosened me and I fly.

But it seem as though I haven't made a nest yet when am I going to rest. I'm only going to last for so long and I feel as though I am not strong. My back is aching and I'm drenched in sweat.

I feel like I have been flying for months and haven't had a break, I need to sit and rest my wings before I pass out because I can't breathe. I need some air, somehow it seems dry.

There is no water or air supply. But I have got to keep flying. I can't stop now. I have made it this far, there's no turning around. But as I fly I wonder have they changed when I left.

Am I missing something? I haven't found what I was looking for yet so I start flying again and wondering about that. But one thing I wonder about is it has to be around.

I can't keep flying to start all over again. Cause one day I won't be able to fly and have to face it then.

FACE THE WORLD **************

God bless my soul for the world.

I have found looks like gold.

Since I beam in this image humble is how I will leave out.

Lead me through a path of righteousness for faith I will have and knowledge I will gain.

HAIR *************

If you can't achieve it just weave it.

Twist, braid and dreads.

Naps a perm to your head wash and condition well dark and lovely works well.

When I'm finished you can tell you hair is healthy and there's a up do on your head.

YOU

It's just the little cute things you do.

I knew when you're around me you don't put the tough man act on.

I start to see your gentle side .

I see a side other people see.

But I also see a side they don't.

They won't understand but I love you and I love the sweet person I know you are.

Like your smile, your humor.

That's why you will always be my boo.

Because they might not think so but I love you and they just don't know how much!

FINDING LOVE

DO YOU KNOW LOVE

Everyone say they know about love.

We all know the definition it's a feeling between two or more people.

We also say that we know the feeling but we don't really know until we have been broken.

There's different types of love.

You can love everybody but you can only be in love with one person.

What a feeling of having that experience.

Love is a job not only a feeling.

It is also an affection that is hard to be broken.

It's hard to find true love.

Love is support, trust, courage, bravery, heart, mind and soul.

It's a dedication to someone.

To be who you are and grow the better for.

Love will stay the same and won't change.

You can't change love you can only change the people you fall in love with.

But sometime your feelings will stay the same.

We use the word so much for play.

That sometimes we miss out on the real thing.

So don't let love pass you by.

Ask yourself do you really know love?

ACROSS MY MIND

From time 2 time you run across my mind.

Old memories start creating an image in my mind.

Yeah times were good, laughing and all.

At the time you were a good friend, at first impression.

Sometimes I want to call you to see how you are doing, to see how everything is going with you.

Just to ask some questions, to start something that is already dead.

I'll think to myself why do I even try to be nice.

It's like I'm trying to find something but don't know what it is.

You answer them still.

Well the last time saw you I realized I didn't feel the same about you.

The feelings were dead, you have been replaced.

It seemed that your story was the same.

I HOPE YOU'RE DOING BETTER.

You just came across my mind one day.

A LETTER OF THANKS TO YOU

When I first say you, you had a smile that could light you the world.

I saw you as just another person and wasn't feeling you then.

Every time you saw me you would stop to say hi.

I knew you liked me but I just wasn't hearing it.

I thought you was like the others, hollering at me for one thing or because you like what you saw in my jeans.

Not seeing or getting to know the loving and caring person inside.

We started talking and I was beginning to fall in love.

Even though was I frontend and hiding my feelings.

Putting you off to the side knowing deep inside you're the one I should be with.

When I finally tool the chance you treated me like a queen ever since.

You warm my heart and give me butterflies.

When you hold me I feel safe.

When you make laugh I feel like a jolly fat kid in a candy store.

When you kiss me I know I have found true love.

I thank you for being there and providing me with your tender love and care.

TOGETHER

There's so many names I can call you to express the way I feel for you.

That I don't know which one to say.

I have went from one step to another.

We have grown from friends to lovers.

Have called each other names like baby to wifey and husband.

Told each other our feelings and the way we felt.

Never had an argument or a fight yet.

Things are going good.

That we can't get each other off of the others mind.

We are just building something that we will try to make last a lifetime.

I'm here for you and you are there for me.

We have a bond together you and me.

We will go through rain and the storm and we will still come out strong.

To prove the love we have for each other is more than words can say.

We pray to God that He Won't break us apart.

That we were each other's soul mates from the start.

Right now we will just grow,

We will grow mentally, physically and emotionally for each other no matter what.

We will come as one.

I WANNA GET CLOSE TO YOU

Your essence is so strong I might find myself doing wrong.

 I want to get close to you.

As heat forms and I try to back up, instead of going forward I find myself wanting to get close to you.

As I see you lick the moist air off your lips and your tight abs I want to grip.

I know I want to get close to you.

When I rub my fingers through your hair and you lay gently on my leg.

As you listen to my heart beat through my belly I think want to get close to you.

I just hope someday I'll get that chance.

Even though this may not be the right time.

Just want to let you know you're on my mind.

My heart is crying out for romance, I want to get close to you if you have the time.

The key is at the door for you to open.

Once you walk in, there Is no need for words, cause I want to get close to you.

LOVING YOU

Loving you is easy to do but staying true is hard for me and you.

Words I can say out my mouth.

But feelings will beat me to the ground.

Things we say to each other day and night, passion we rage in the speed of light.

Our feelings we share in joy and rain.

The only one I can talk to who feels my pain.

Hearts pure and warm brought together.

Adored in the eye sight of God.

Growing through hard times and trouble to test our strength of growth.

Wisdom and knowledge we gain, learning form one another and experiences we have together.

A bond we have that no one can share.

A part of each other like Adam and Eve.

Knowing my thoughts, when you know what I'm about to say.

The one I run to in the morning and night.

The one I cry about when he's not doing right.

The stuff I go through, holding on to you with might.

Knowing what to do and the words to say to brighten up my day.

Love is a word that's about us but the definition we can't explain.

Being with you is what I have to question, cause the love we have

is everlasting between me and you.

Through sickness and health our love will never perish because we love each other to death.

I SEE RIGHT THROUGH YOU

You're nice to talk 2.

You understand where I'm coming from.

When I tell you what's on my mind.

I like it when you hold me.

Just the warm attention that goes over me.

How you make me laugh by the things you say and when you tickle me.

I feel like I'm a kid again.

How you kiss my head gently.

Your hand massaging my back.

I feel relaxed and free.

Just the warm good feeling we have together.

 It's almost like you're watching a movie.

I miss those days and those times.

If only we do that right now.

Cause you always know what to do to put me in a good mood.

I like how you rock yourself to sleep cause I rock with you.

Just the little cute things you do. I know you are around me you can't put the tough man out

And I start to see the side other people see.

But I also see a side they don't.

They won't understand but I love you and I love the sweet person I know you are. I like your smile, your humor.

That's why you always be my boo.

Because they might not think so but I love you and they don't just don't know how much.

NEW SOMEONE

I found a new someone.

It seems good now but will t turn out to be a lifetime.

I thought my old one was going to be 4 ever but turns out it was just me and the love I had for him.

Hopeful this is a start of what I was waiting for.

I will see a new beginning and more happy and joyful times.

It is not new when I can't say I tried but not now my someone is mine.

THE ONE

You are an angle that I have prayed for and thought I had.

I realize now that I was just blind by the image that I thought I had my soul mate.

Not saying he was a bad person but he wasn't the one.

The one that has opened my eyes.

The one that share the same things I like.

The one that gives ne butterflies when I look in your eyes.

The one that speaks through his heart as well as mine.

The one who can see what I see.

The one I see as my best friend, I can tell anything as well as my lover.

The one that can't stand to see me sad.

The one who brighten up my day, who put sparkles in my eyes and a blush on my face.

The one I thought I would have later in life when I'm older.

But thank God everyday he sent my gift early.

I pray that we will have future together and get married but if anything happens and that's not a part of the plan, I will like to say thank for being a friend, lover and my angle for the time.

And we will always share these memories that no one can take apart.

But I hope our future holds a lifetime.

MY LOVE

The first time I met you I felt something strange. I knew I had to have you, because I've never felt this way before, you gave me a certain feeling as I looked at you across the way. Ever since then it hasn't been the same. I can't explain it. The warm, loving, caring touch you give me as a lover should, when I'm with you. It's funny, cause we have been through the same things, the storm and the rain. We have both cried a tear of pain. You have the answers to the questions I have asked. Day and night I have learned new things from you. You've shown me such a beautiful sight of love as we stood under the moon light. You have added too what I have always wanted. We have shared something that I've always dreamed of, we share love mentally , physically and spiritually. This is something no one can ever take from us. You have been my sunshine in the morning and my angel in the sky. I will cry for days if you were to ever leave my side. I have fallen in love with you in such little time. You are my earth, moon and shinning -star. I'm just telling you how I feel because what I feel for you Is real. Like I said you're my fairy tale prince in a Cinderella story. I'm smiling inside and out that I have one of my own. You know what to say to make me happy, knowing how to put a smile on my face. Like the song writer has sang in her song, "You are the truth" You are so real and I love the way you make me feel. Now that I have you everything has changed and I can see more clearly now. To the words of this song, I can identify, and I will promise to love you, show you love and will not leave you because my love for you is real!

MY BOO

You have touched me in a way you really don't know.

I'm still surprised by what you have shown me.

I smile every time I think of you.

I like how you make me laugh just to see me smile.

When you hold me close I feel your heart beating, knowing I'm loved.

You're fun to hang out with and we have grown so close.

We both like the same things, that's why my feelings for you have grown.

I have experienced some new things since we have been together.

It's nice to be in love.

Some can't relate to what I have with you.

That's why it's a blessing from above.

I know you say that you're blessed all the time, but I have been blessed since the day you became mine.

I hope I make you as happy as you have made me.

No matter what happens, no one can take what we have shared.

I'm here for you whenever you need me as a lover and a friend.

IN YOUR EYES

In your eyes I see something new.

I see a image of me in side of you.

When your eyes I see a light when the sun shines on you.

In your eyes I see beauty, the beauty of a heart that loves me so.

In your eyes I see faith, the faith you hold strong to make us grow.

In your eyes I see fire the fire that makes passion flow.

In your eyes I see a caring person that won't hurt a soul.

In your eyes I see precaution while you wait to see my face.

In your eyes I see something sweet as you say something sweet to me.

In your eyes I see laughter, that you spread to brighten up my day.

In your eyes is see your love and me falling for you.

I REMEMBER YOU

I remember you standing outside.

The first time I saw you, you greeted me with words so kind.

As your warm brown eyes looked into mine.

You said hello as the corners of your mouth went into a smile.

Everyone knew you, cause they said hello while passing by.

I knew from then on you were a special guy.

You inspired a lot of people with your strong words and have always been a friend one could count on.

You feel people with laughter and their hearts with grace.

Teaching people things people never thought of, as you welcome them into this place.

Now things aren't the same since you're gone.

I still remember you standing with a smile knowing today the sun will shine on another good day and that everything would be alright.

I know you're still smiling now, looking down on us.

I still won't forget the good times.

I will always remember you and your big smile.

SOMETHING SWEET

You're so very sweet.

Your words and smile is sweet as a strawberry.

I like your pecan brown eyes.

Your chocolate like a sneakers bar.

I want to take a bite that's how good you are.

Your fresh and clean like outcast said.

Smooth as a baby's bottom.

The lady's man you say.

You make me laugh with your funny faces.

You hold me in your arms with passion.

Calling to see where I am at when I'm not around.

Your warm as a blanket. Fine as a prince.

Every time you kiss me my eyes light up.

Your lips are as sweet as bubble gum.

Every time you pop it.

You are something sweet my prince.

ME & YOU

Me and you are one of a kind.

But there's something that runs through my mind.

I don't know if I love you the same.

It's just that some things have changed.

I don't know if I'm on your mind all the time.

But it seems like you just fade away.

Maybe it's just but I get tired of the same thing.

Time to step up with some game!

I'm not old like Mary.

I'm young and don't have time for games.

I don't know what this will come too but I hope you come up with something new, to bring back me and you.

HAVING LOVE

I thought I really knew you but don't know if I'm ready for you.

Your to string and you take over a person's heart and mind.

You make us go crazy and loose our minds, we feel as if we are floating in the sky.

Sometimes we forget about what's real and important.

That's if we are really into you.

See you're so powerful that I feel you have an impression on me but I really can't tell.

Right now I think I'm fooling myself because I know what's it like to have a part of you.

It's a beautiful feeling that you don't want to let go.

I can only wait to see if it's my time.

At that time I will know if it's really you love.

LOVE OF MY LIFE

What can I say about you?

You're more than words that could possibly come from my mouth, yet can only come from my heart.

You're my best friend. We talk about any and everything.

I talk to you about things I sometimes can't talk to my girls about.

We don't argue about things when we get mad.

We talk all of our problems out and make up about it.

We laugh and goof around all the time.

Like you said, I'm your half and you are mine.

We make one!

We have been through things but have remained together no matter what people have said we have been strong., because we love other, letting anyone break us apart.

You have been my support and helping hand.

We are support for each other in everything we do.

Everything is going to turn out good for us.

I'm happy you are mine and that I am yours.

You're the love of my life and I love you!

SOMEONE SPECIAL

I have learned a lot from you ever since we've been together.

I learned about love, how to love and how to love myself.

I'm learning about love and that I will always have someone to count on, someone that will answer all of my questions.

I admire you in so many ways.

I admire your strength, like whenever you fall you always get back up.

I admire your courage.

You don't settle for the word no, always striving for excellence.

I admire your pride in whatever you're doing.

I realize god has blessed me in so many ways and of one those blessings is you!

I'm blessed to say that I have you now, and whatever happens I will always be around.

I have learned a lot from the things you have shown me, like just what this life has to offer.

You've shown me how to connect with my spiritual life as well as the physical side.

A lot of people haven't realized just how much they can touch a person's life such as you have touched mine.

You're my best friend and lover and I will always love you even until the end...............

FIRST KISS

First- it happens before everything else.

It's mostly the word before.

In racing it's like the grand prize.

Kissing happens when two people put their lips together.

A first kiss is when a boy falls in love with a girl, that's his gift.

A first gift is a reminder of all of the other kisses.

It's like playing double Dutch, wanting to get to the top.

It's like learning a new game that you have finally gotten the hang of.

That's when you get your first kiss.

HAVING CONFLICT

GAME

It's funny how you think you're in love with someone and you're really not.

One feeling you thought you had you did not.

One's love is really a friend and things didn't happen like you thought it should have.

One person you thought you would have been with to the end.

Before you knew it, they left you at the beginning.

You thought you were in love from the things on your mind.

Because it was your first thought.

You couldn't tell what your heart was saying.

Feelings you had then you don't have anymore.

How can you tell if what you feel is real when what you feel is gone.

Then you feel the same things for another.

Will it be the same. Were you rushing into things?

Or just count up the game.

The game that's so strong you don't know where you begin and where you end.

Now you see that you let the game take control.

So it's your turn to take over the game.

The game of love is something true or can it be used?

Whatever you do, you can let it hurt you

DEAR?

I have wrote you and wrote you and waited for your call.

I haven't heard from you and we haven't gotten in touch at all.

I want to know if you're alright and what's going on.

But when I try to call you I just get a dial tone.

There's a lot of catching up to do and we haven't started yet.

I have a lot of questions to ask you and I'm starting to forget.

There's a lot I have to tell you and I don't know what to begin with.

I hope this letter reaches you, if it doesn't I guess it's good bye.

At least I tried to get in touch with you.

So won't you?

I DON'T KNOW

You got me thinking to myself that things have changed.

I'm getting that feeling again.

That feeling that I have had many times before.

That I'm not feeling him anymore.

That excitement and spark started to leave.

I know me and I'm the type of person where I can't stand doing the same thing for long.

I have to try something new every once in a while.

If I'm doing the same thing all the time it seems like I'm a robot and that's just something I'm not.

I know you're trying but like you need attention too.

If I feel like I'm not getting it anymore my mind starts to search for it.

I start to give it if I see I can get it.

I started buying you things, depending and leaning on you hand and foot.

But now I feel like you shutting me out.

You now doing the things you used to do.

I know it's not always going to be the same at a period of all that go-ing to change.

As the relationship go on you feel you don't have to do those things any-more, you already have me.

But what me fell to remember they can be irreplaceable.

I love you, you better than any boyfriend.

I have had but it's time for a change.

This may always be there but if other things, you let me I will be there if it might leave and so will I.

DO YOU LOVE ME

You say U love me but do you like you say you do.

I don't feel your touch or see the happiness in your smile.

Are you really wearing a frown underneath?

Do your kisses have a meaning.

Do you see my face when you're dreaming.

When you see my picture do you get butterflies inside.

Do you think about me all the time when I am not around.

Do I remind you of little things you happen to come upon.

Do you talk about me constantly and call to say that I am on your mind.

Do you hunger for your body to rub up against minded, for your lips to press softly against mine, do you have my picture everywhere and always by your side.

Do your eyes sparkle because I look like an Angel in the sky.

Do you pray on your knees and say thank you god for giving her to me.

If you do all of these things, then I know you truly love me.

CONNECTION

I tried to find it. I looked and looked for that certain connection.

I wanted to feel that special thing that put butterflies in your stomach and you're on a cloud floating away.

I felt it at first, it seemed like it was getting there.

But I think I was trying too hard. Because it went away.

I even closed my eyes to feel like I was in another place.

But for some reason it won't go that way.

I know I can't force it. It has to come to me.

It only comes at a special time when there are certain feelings between you and me.

I feel you're in my heart so I know it's love.

When we kiss I want to feel that too.

I want to feel that spark that connected us into two.

I want to feel your inside feelings of love.

I want to feel a part of you and how happy I make you.

I want to see that sparkle I your eyes that can light up the sky.

That certain connection that make us lovers.

PASSION

HELD

He held me in his arms tight.

His strong arms around my waste.

His head pressed to my heart.

I feel like I am a baby in my mothers' arms and she's rocking me to sleep.

I feel loved and cared for like can't no one harm me.

I feel held.

FIRE

It's 100 degrees sweat coming from my face.

My legs are shaking.

My head went back as my nails went into his back..............

The covers flower like waves as the heat if our bodies pressed against them.

My eyes closed tighter the pain grew and the emotions went deeper and deeper.

Echo's' in the room got louder.

The moist in the heat formed a bond.

The pain began to feel better when the passion took over me.

He held me closer and closer , moving backward then forward in a slow motion.

I was in another world as he down below.

I felt the tingle in my spin and I knew this wasn't going to be the last time.

I'm breathing hard.

Minutes are turning into hours till something came up out of me and I never felt the same.

This fire has been lit!

I WANT YOU

It's something you should know and I'm feeling like I'm running out of time to tell you.

As the day passes and daylight turns into night, I sit there sometimes wanting my phone to ring s I can hear your voice on the other end.

If you only knew the feelings I have right now.

I want to talk to you to get some things off my mind.

I realize that you understand and even though we have had our up's and downs, you were there to help me through a lot and remained by my side.

But what you don't know is I need you and still have love for you.

My love for you never went away.

I was just fronting and hiding my feelings inside.

Maybe it's too late for that now but I know you feel the same way.

I hear it in your voice and others can tell by the look in your eyes.

If I can't get another chance than I hope you can be my helping hand.

I just hope I can let you know that I want you and will never let you go.

MISSING YOU

As I sit and look at the moon and the ocean view.

I sit here thinking of how I miss you.

Looking at the waves imagining your smile, missing how you used to hold me in your arms.

How that warm feeling went through me, making me feel free.

The moon glooming on a beautiful night, wishing we were in that site holding hands as we walked the sands of the beach under our feet.

Thinking of the days we spent I'm thinking of how we will meet.

Walking alone wishing you were with me.

You're warm face and big tight hugs making me feel like a princess.

All I can think of is how I miss you!

I'm just missing you.

VIBE

I feel like a strong muscle in my thighs.

The room sis dark as you hear a vibration flowing through the air.

The air is thick and it's hard to breath because the heat of these bodies making if feel like 100 degrees.

Sweat over flowing but it feels like cool water to my skin.

This tight dress is clinging to me and my feet hurt in these heals.

I don't show the pain, because beauty is pain when you're looking this good.

As I sway my hips from side to side and my backside is going up and down, I find myself moving into the rhythm and the view in your eyes are telling me that yes you are feeling me.

The devilish grin on your face is saying you like what you see.

These wide hips, full breast, small waste and caramel completion.

A phenomenal beauty! What a treat! I don't pay you any attention because this music has taken over me.

I feel like I'm flying and no one can bring me down but me.

The sweet ecstasy of music is a strong melody.

It's nice to feel free.

BEAUTIFUL

Beautiful, that's what we had shared.

Laughter, joy, passion and happiness.

You made me feel like I was in the sky. High on cloud 9.

Taking me out to dinner, opening doors, going to the movies.

We played together, talked about everything.

Knew and understood how the other felt.

Knowing how to speak to one another about our problems.

You were like my home girl and I was like your homie.

Best friends.

Beautiful it what we had.

What happened to that beautiful thing and why do I feel like it's going to end.

I hope I'm wrong because It doesn't have to be this way.

What we have is still beautiful, I just want it to stay that way.

I hope it will never change.

It was beautiful in the beginning and beautiful it shall remain.

IN THE NIGHT

My passion hungered for him.

As I felt his dark strong brown arms go around me.

I carved his image as he eased inside of me.

The pain of love flowed like a sea under a full moon in a dark gloomy night.

A new world was over me. I was free from love, care and passion all my dark side effects were erased.

I flew deeper and deeper as it over me.

His love healed me with his care bond over me.

I was in a box.

It was something I never experienced before

HURT

WHY

Why I love you so much when o worry so much.

Why do I call so often when you're doing the same.

Why am I getting my hopes up, feeling joyful only for you to make me fall.

Why do I keep running to you, saying that you're going to change.

Yet all you do is run away, giving me pain.

Why do I fall in midst of your holes only to become stuck like you, having only anger to hold.

Why do I let you get the best of me when all you do is hurt me.

ANOTHER

I love you but I can't tell you the truth.

I have feelings for another and I don't know what to do.

The rage of temptation has made me cheat on you.

Guilty lips pressed against his as I thought of you.

The pain of a broken heart took over as I talked to you.

Feeling lonely and distressed made me reach for another's hand to put my heart at rest.

The barren heart is full with pain and has struck me to death.

I feel no love and to be sentenced to death.

How can I love when I have no love for myself.

The touch of his arm and the passion of his eyes made me want to go further but the little piece inside of me wouldn't let me.

Now I am ashamed and to be your lover again.

But I still have these feelings for another.

The problem is that you don't know.

REVENGE

You have hurt me and you don't even know.

It never crossed your mind that you are doing me wrong.

I haven't told you how I feel.

We haven't talked in a while so my lips have been sealed.

You came and got your package, left.

Going back to your normal routine.

Like nothing even happened.

I have found a new face to replace the thought of seeing yours.

He's cool. I wasn't feeling him at first, thinking he was lame.

But then I started talking to him more and my feelings changed.

O got greedy in my anger and began looking for more.

I found out it was fun.

Besides you act like you don't care anymore.

Then a thought came to me, that this is wrong.

I tried to cut them off, but then I felt like I didn't give a f*** anymore.

I did a lot for you.

But you're not acknowledging that fact.

My patience is getting weaker while this revenge is getting sweeter.

I found myself at his place.

These arms that once held you was around his waist.

These lips that said I love you were now in his face.

The fact that I was guilty, I feel like I was in the right place.

I love you but the hunger for revenge was taking over my place.

LOST

I'm lost with you and wondering if I'm missing something being with you.

I regret the first time I let you.

But will do it again.

I feel you are giving up on us day by day.

You're making false promises and your talk is not the same.

As my mind wonders my heart is still saying the same thing.

But sometimes it wonders also when you give me pain.

O put my feelings aside and hold it in the midst of my anger that is spilled onto another.

As I come to you t tell you how I feel my emotions close like sealed lips faced upon fear and a false smile full of joy is there to comfort you.

To tell you you're right and there by your side.

When in my mind I'm tired of wondering and why do I have to go through this again.

But yet you don't understand and I feel you have taken me for granted.

Your eyes are in space and you don't see the tears that are coming from you're lover's face.

Or have your love for me been replaced by another's touch and comfort.

Am I just here when you need a smile.

All I do is just sit think of a better place and can I get there if I break free.

Because right now I'm lost.

Will you please just help me.

GO

Here we go again.

The same o'll mess.

Why do I have to go through this.

I'm tired of this. I want to just throw something at the wall or just punch the wall myself.

It's just when I don't feel like talking, don't feel like looking at no one.

 Don't want to be happy.

I just want to leave and go somewhere by myself.

I don't feel like being bothered.

Leave me alone. Don't ask me anything.

Don't ask me to do anything for you just leave me alone!!!

Let me be by myself.

Sometimes I just feel like starting by myself again or to do something like running away.

I don't know, I just want to go.

When will I ever get out!

Now I know I know why people commit suicide.

BROKEN

My heart is broken by the sadness of being a part.

Something that I have has been taken away from me.

I sit again in depression, anger and aloneness.

Every time I think I have to give back something that I cherish as a real treasure, it perishes.

Gone right before my eyes.

I try to open my heart and trust but am confused not knowing who to trust.

It never fails.

They do they always have to hurt me.

Did I do something?

I love.

I'm happy one second sad the next.

I have nothing else to say. Just pass me by.

2 SIDES

You are mad and frustrated with anger.

I'm quit and scared with fear.

You come in my mind with a spirit of hurt also a image of dong wrong.

 I stay still because

I want to do no harm.

You are a rage and want everything your way.

If not then you are depressed and can't do anything.

I understand there will be a next time.

There's no need for pain.

You don't do things right and always trying to put yourself down.

I am strong.

I don't worry about what people say.

I'll still carry on. I'm beautiful anyway!

You hurt people's feelings and call them names, I try to make everyone happy and if I don't than I'll bring myself down.

You are sour always having some type of drama to bring.

I try not to let that get in my way.

You will still be with me.

I will have to face that fact because you are a part of me.

Just the other half.

LOSING YOU

If you had the choice of losing someone would you take it or back down.

Having to see someone suffer because your heart can't take the pain of seeing them leaving.

Thinking of the time you spent as a child. Growing up together.

Knowing that person is still alive.

The person who used to make you laugh, gave you wisdom and knowledge.

The one who called you nicknames and would go to the store just to give you money or to buy you candy.

Showing you how much they loved you.

As you look at that person and think about all those things, you never thought this would happen.

Yet God works in mysterious ways.

You will never know when you should leave or stay.

All you can do is think, should I pull the plug or let it stay.

BURN

A part of me is telling me this is the end.

That you don't love me anymore.

You're just here for one thing.

It was all good in the beginning but how we have fallen apart.

You don't call like you used to and the words get shorter every time we speak.

The other part of me is telling me maybe it's me.

You just really don't have the time.

I just need to be patient right now.

You still have love for me but you are really busy.

Besides, my heart already belongs to you.

I love you to death even though I try to make it go away.

I thought maybe I was just fooling myself but the truth will always come out in the end.

I can't change the way my heart feels.

I also can't sit here and hurt again.

So maybe I just have to let it burn.

THE END

It has come to an end my love.

We have to let this relationship go.

But don't want to let it burn.

I just want to make it grow.

We have been through a lot together.

Both have shed some tears, fighting through haters.

But now we have come to an end.

It's hard to let something go that you love the most.

But you know it's not going to work out so you have to move forth.
If only it didn't have to be this way.

My heart is calling you but deep within I am feeling pain and you can't meet me half way.

My eyes start to water as the tears began to fall from the things that go through my mind.

I will cry for days cause the love from my heart is still running through my veins.

My heart drops and the butterflies started a rage.

I feel like I am lost, in the first stage of depression.

I'm falling in the sorrow of loneliness.

My heart has shifted away and I'm still PMSING about everything.

You're still in my mind and still in my dreams.

I know I love you because you were a part of me.

My shoulder to lean on, the one who understands me and where I am coming from when others were lost.

But I know it's ok because you're still inside of me.

No one can ever take your place even though it has come to an end.

My love you still hold your space.

www.ingramcontent.com/pod-product-compliance
Lightning Source LLC
Chambersburg PA
CBHW060515030426
42337CB00015B/1897